Editor
Lorin Klistoff, M.A.

Editorial Manager
Karen J. Goldfluss, M.S. Ed.

Editor-in-Chief
Sharon Coan, M.S. Ed.

Cover Artist
Jessica Orlando

Art Coordinator
Denice Adorno

Creative Director
Elayne Roberts

Imaging
James Edward Grace
Stephanie A. Salcido

Product Manager
Phil Garcia

Publishers
Rachelle Cracchiolo, M.S. Ed.
Mary Dupuy Smith, M.S. Ed.

How to Ca Measurements

Grades 3–4

Author
Robert Smith

Teacher Created Materials, Inc.
6421 Industry Way
Westminster, CA 92683
www.teachercreated.com

ISBN-1-57690-486-5

©2000 Teacher Created Materials, Inc.
Reprinted, 2003
Made in U.S.A.

Table of Contents

How to •••••••••••••••••••••• Use This Book

A Note to Teachers and Parents

Welcome to the "How to" math series! You have chosen one of over two dozen books designed to give your children the information and practice they need to acquire important concepts in specific areas of math. The goal of the "How to" math books is to give children an extra boost as they work toward mastery of the math skills established by the National Council of Teachers of Mathematics (NCTM) and outlined in grade-level scope and sequence guidelines.

The design of this book is intended to allow it to be used by teachers or parents for a variety of purposes and needs. Each of the units contains one or more "How to" pages and two or more practice pages. The "How to" section of each unit precedes the practice pages and provides needed information such as a concept or math rule review, important terms and formulas to remember, or step-by-step guidelines necessary for using the practice pages. While most "How to" pages are written for direct use by the children, in some lower-grade level books these pages are presented as instructional pages or direct lessons to be used by a teacher or parent prior to introducing the practice pages.

About This Book

How to Calculate Measurements: Grades 3–4 presents a comprehensive overview of measurement for students at this level. It can be used to introduce and teach basic measurement to children with little or no background in the concepts.

The units in this book can be used in whole-class instruction with the teacher or by a parent assisting his or her child through the book. This book also lends itself to use by a small group doing remedial or review work on measurement or for individuals and small groups in earlier grades engaged in enrichment or accelerated work. A teacher may want to have two tracks within his or her class with one moving at a faster pace and the other at a gradual pace appropriate to the ability or background of the children. This book can also be used in a learning center containing materials needed for each unit of instruction.

Children should be allowed to use a calculator to check computations. Other materials needed for this book include the following: ruler, yardstick, meter stick, thermometer, and protractor. Encourage children to use manipulatives to reinforce the concepts introduced in this book. Children should practice measuring or weighing objects whenever possible. Seize the moment and have children use an object such as a penny, a toy block, or a pencil to measure the number of units around a piece of paper, the dimensions of a desk, or the length and width of a door frame. Have children hold two objects and decide which weighs more.

If children have difficulty with a specific concept or unit within this book, review the material and allow them to redo the troublesome pages. Since concept development in these units is sequential, it is not advisable to skip units. It is preferable for children to find the work easy at first and to gradually advance to the more difficult concepts.

How to Calculate Measurements: Grades 3–4 highlights the use of various measuring devices and activities and emphasizes the development of proficiency in the use of basic measurement facts and processes for doing measuring. It provides a wide variety of instructional models and explanations for the gradual and thorough development of measuring concepts and processes. The units in this book are designed to match the suggestions of the National Council of Teachers of Mathematics (NCTM). They strongly support the learning of measurement and other processes in the context of problem solving and real-world applications. Use every opportunity to have students apply these new skills in classroom situations and at home. This will reinforce the value of the skill as well as the process.

How to Calculate Measurements: Grades 3–4 matches a number of NCTM standards including the following main topics and specific features:

Measurements

The study of mathematics should include measurement in many facets. This book encourages and guides the use of measuring tools and the development of the actual processes of measurement as they relate to length, capacity, weight, area, perimeter, time, temperature, and angle. The text stresses understanding and using the units of measurement and making and estimating measurements across many aspects of measurement. It also emphasizes practical applications for everyday living.

Problem Solving

The study of mathematics should emphasize problem solving in such a way that students can use problem-solving approaches to investigate and understand the general content of mathematics. In this book, students are encouraged to solve problems involving everyday situations and real-life applications of math skills as they relate to measurements.

Communication

This workbook includes numerous opportunities for students to apply diagrams, charts, and measurement tools to concrete mathematical ideas. Students can relate their everyday common language to the expression of mathematical ideas and symbols on a level appropriate to their age. They can communicate the results of their measurement experiences with each other.

Reasoning

This book helps students apply logic to their math problems and asks them to justify their answers. There is an emphasis on recognizing patterns as a way of applying the units of measurement and the processes of measurement as well as the use of models, measurement manipulatives, and charts.

Connections

Throughout the book, students are encouraged to recognize and relate various measurement concepts, processes, and patterns to each other and to other mathematical concepts. They are likewise encouraged to use measurement in science and in their daily lives.

Other Standards

The pages in this book are also well aligned with other NCTM standards which stress instruction of whole number computation, estimation, and geometrical concepts through real-life applications. This book also stresses that fractions, decimals, and math patterns be taught or reinforced with real-life and hands-on applications.

Facts to Know

A ruler is the most common measuring instrument most people use. It is very important to understand how to use a ruler.

- A ruler is 1 foot long. It is divided into 12 inches.

- Each inch ends at the long line to the right of the number. Each inch is divided into smaller parts.

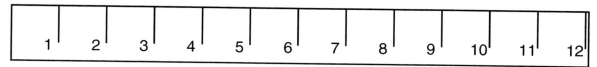

- The half-inch mark is exactly halfway between each number. Half-inch marks are the next longest lines.

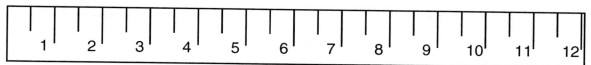

- The quarter inch marks show ¼ of an inch and ¾ of an inch. The quarter-inch marks are the next longest lines.

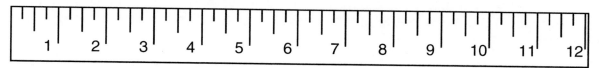

- Always begin measuring from the left end of the ruler. In the illustration below, the marker is 6½ inches long.

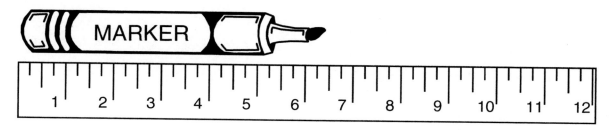

A yardstick is another common measuring instrument most people use. It is also very important to understand how to use a yardstick. A yardstick is 3 feet long.

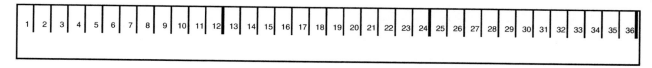

- A yardstick is the length of 3 rulers. It is divided into 36 inches.

- A yardstick is used to measure the length of larger or longer objects. A football field is exactly 100 yards long.

Directions: Use a ruler to measure the length of each of the objects illustrated below.

1.

_____

3.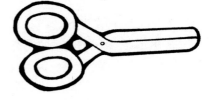

_____

2.

_____

4.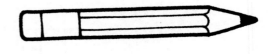

_____

Directions: Choose four small objects from your desk, classroom, or pocket to measure with a ruler. Write down the name of the object, outline it, and record the measurement to the nearest quarter, half, or inch mark.

5. Object: _____

   Length: _____

6. Object: _____

   Length: _____

7. Object: _____

   Length: _____

8. Object: _____

   Length: _____

① Practice ···· Using a Yardstick and a Meter Stick

A yardstick is exactly 3 feet, or 36 inches, long.

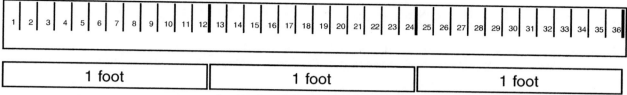

| 1 foot | 1 foot | 1 foot |

1 yard = 3 feet = 36 inches

A meter stick is about 3 inches longer than a yardstick. It is 100 centimeters long.

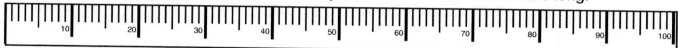

1 meter = 100 centimeters

To measure large objects, follow these steps:

1. Place the yardstick (or meter stick) at one end of the object.

2. Use chalk to mark the end of the stick.

3. Place the stick on the chalk line.

4. Keep a record of how many yards (or meters) have been measured.

5. Round the last part of the measurement to the nearest yard (or meter).

Directions: Measure the following objects with a yardstick or meter stick. Round your answers to the nearest yard or meter.

1. the length of the school basketball court

   _____ yards (or meters)

2. the longest side of the handball court

   _____ yards (or meters)

3. the length of the volleyball court

   _____ yards (or meters)

4. the length of the hopscotch game

   _____ yards (or meters)

5. the distance from home plate to first base on the baseball diamond

   _____ yards (or meters)

6. the length of the path from your classroom to the office

   _____ yards (or meters)

7. the length of your classroom

   _____ yards (or meters)

8. the width of your classroom

   _____ yards (or meters)

9. the length of the playground

   _____ yards (or meters)

10. the width of the playground

   _____ yards (or meters)

Directions: Use a ruler to measure the following items. Use a light pencil mark to mark the end of the ruler if the measurement is longer than one ruler. Mark your answer to the nearest inch.

1. the length of your desk _____ inches

2. the width of your desk _____ inches

3. the length of your math book _____ inches

4. the width of your math book _____ inches

5. the length of your arm from fingertips to the elbow _____ inches

6. the length of your shoe _____ inches

Directions: Use a ruler and the information on page 5 to measure each of the items below to the nearest half inch.

7. the length of your index finger

_____ inches

8. the length of your pencil

_____ inches

9. the width (shorter side) of your paper

_____ inches

10. the length of a crayon or marker

_____ inches

Facts to Know

U.S. Customary Units

- A ruler is 1 foot long. A foot is divided into 12 inches.
- Each inch is divided into 2 half inches.
- Each inch is divided into 4 quarter inches.
- Each inch is divided into 8 eighth inches.

  Study the markings on this part of the ruler.

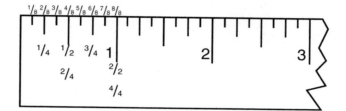

- The abbreviation for foot is *ft.* or ´. The abbreviation for inch is *in.* or ". The piece of chalk shown here is $\frac{7}{8}$ of an inch long ($\frac{7}{8}$ in. or $\frac{7}{8}$").

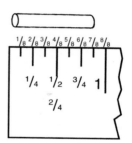

Metric Units

Many rulers show both customary and metric units. The edge opposite the inch markings is divided into metric units. Metric units are often used in science. They are helpful in precisely measuring smaller objects. Because metric units are based on the number 10, it is often easier to do mathematical computation with metric measurement.

- The basic unit of metric measure is the *meter*. A meter is slightly longer than a yard.

- A meter is evenly divided into 100 units called *centimeters*.

- A centimeter is evenly divided into 10 units called *millimeters*.

- The abbreviation for centimeters is *cm*. The abbreviation for millimeters is *mm*.

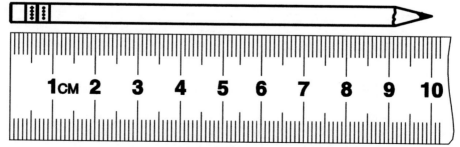

The pencil is 10 centimeters, or 100 millimeters, long.

Directions: Use a ruler and the information on pages 5 and 9 to measure each of the items illustrated below to the nearest eighth of an inch.

1.

the length of this pencil _____

2.

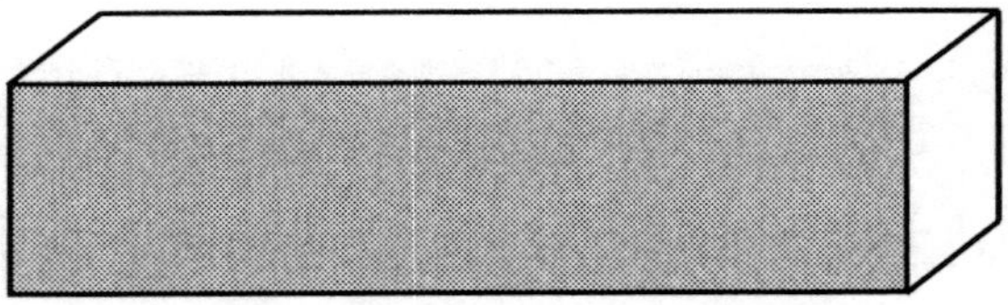

the length of the shaded side
of this block _____

3.  ▬ ▬ ▬ ▬ ▬ ▬ ▬ ▬ ▬ ▬

the length of this dashed line _____

4.

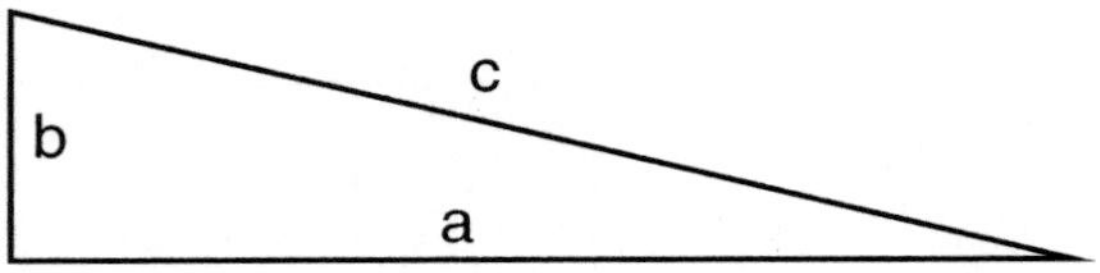

b

c

a

the length of side a _____

$\frac{1}{8}$ $\frac{3}{8}$ $\frac{5}{8}$ $\frac{7}{8}$ | 1 | 2 | 3 | 4 | 5 | 6
$\frac{2}{8}$ $\frac{6}{8}$
$\frac{1}{4}$ $\frac{4}{8}$ $\frac{3}{4}$
$\frac{2}{4}$
$\frac{1}{2}$

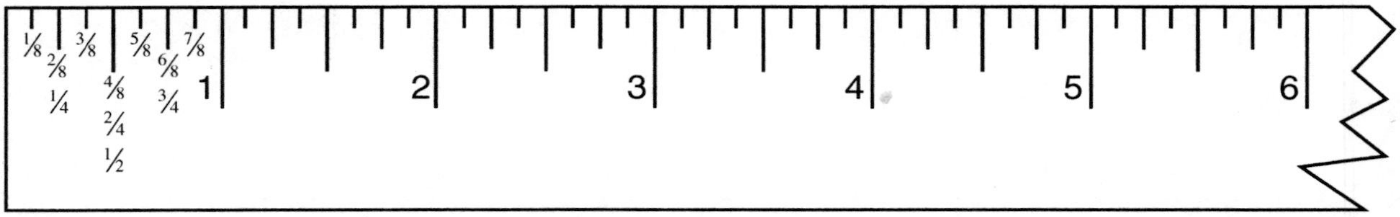

Directions: Use the information on pages 5 and 9 and your ruler to measure each of the objects listed below.

5. the length of a marker

_____ inches

6. the width of a box of tissues

_____ inches

7. the length of your pencil

_____ inches

8. the length of a pair of scissors

_____ inches

9. the length of your hair

_____ inches

10. the length of a paper clip

_____ inches

11. the width of a book

_____ inches

12. the width of a door

_____ inches

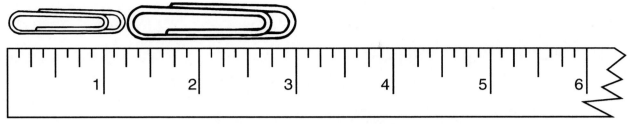

small paper clip   large paper clip

1 ¼ inches   +   1 ³⁄₄ inches = 3 inches

Directions: Use a ruler to measure the items illustrated below. Add the two fractional measurements in each problem.

1. the length of the wrench and the hammer

_____ inches   +   _____ inches   =   _____ inches

2. the length of the two rectangles

_____ inches   +   _____ inches   =   _____ inches

3. the length of the fish and the eel

_____ inches   +   _____ inches   =   _____ inches

Directions: Subtract the length of the first object from the length of the second object. Write the answer in the blanks.

4. the handle of a screwdriver from the whole screwdriver

_____ - _____ = _____

5. the length of the eraser from the length of the pencil

_____ - _____ = _____

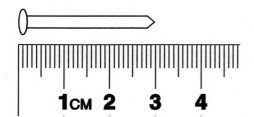

This nail is 3 centimeters long. It is also 30 millimeters long, because a centimeter is divided evenly into 10 millimeters.

Directions: Measure the objects illustrated below. Write the number of centimeters and the number of millimeters for each object.

1. This stick is
   _____ centimeters.
   _____ millimeters.

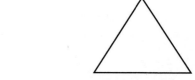

3. The base (bottom) of this triangle is
   _____ centimeters.
   _____ millimeters.

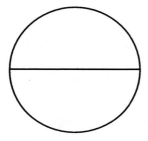

2. The diameter (distance across) of this circle is
   _____ centimeters.
   _____ millimeters.

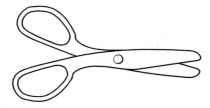

4. The length of these scissors is
   _____ centimeters.
   _____ millimeters.

Directions: Use the grasshopper pictured here to answer these questions. Measure to the nearest centimeter or millimeter.

5. The length of the whole grasshopper is
   _____ centimeters.
   _____ millimeters.

6. The length of the grasshopper's antenna is
   _____ centimeters.
   _____ millimeters.

7. The length of the grasshopper's rear leg is
   _____ centimeters.
   _____ millimeters.

8. The length of the grasshopper's wing is
   _____ centimeters.
   _____ millimeters.

Facts to Know

- Perimeter is the distance around all the edges of an object.
- The fence around a property, such as a house, lot, or a school yard, is the perimeter of the property.
- These words usually indicate perimeter: border, walls, fence, edges, sides, or distance around.

Perimeter of Rectangles

The perimeter of a rectangle can be computed by any of the following ways:
- adding up all four sides of the rectangle
- adding the length and width and multiplying by 2
- using the formula: **P = (l + w) x 2 or P = 2(l + w)**
  (*Note:* P = perimeter, l = length, and w = width)

Compute the perimeter of this rectangle. The length is 7 meters and the width is 5 meters.

Add the 7 meters plus 5 meters which equals 12 meters. Multiply by 2 to include the other two sides of the rectangle. The total is 24 meters.

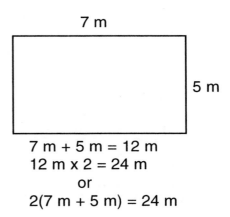

7 m + 5 m = 12 m
12 m x 2 = 24 m
or
2(7 m + 5 m) = 24 m

Perimeter of Other Polygons

Add the sides of each polygon to compute the perimeter.

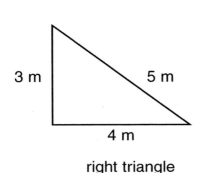

right triangle

3 m + 4 m + 5 m = 12 m
The perimeter is 12 meters.

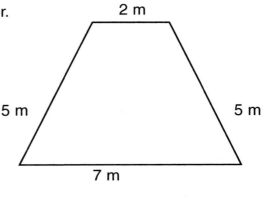

trapezoid

5 m + 2 m + 5 m + 7 m = 19 m
The perimeter is 19 meters.

To compute the perimeter of a rectangle, add the length and the width and then multiply by 2.

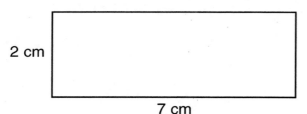

Add 7 cm + 2 cm = 9 cm, then multiply 9 cm x 2 = 18 cm. The perimeter is 18 centimeters.

Directions: Use the information on page 13 to help you compute the perimeter of these rectangles. Remember to label the unit of measurement—inches, feet, yards, meters—in your answer.

1.

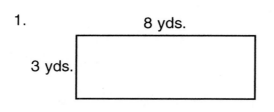

_____

2.

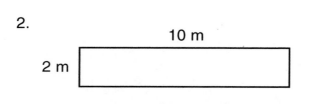

_____

3.

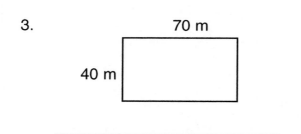

_____

4.

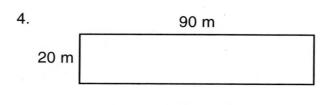

_____

5.

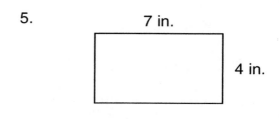

_____

6.

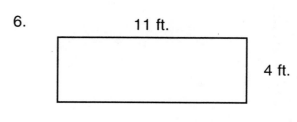

_____

7.

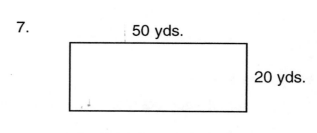

_____

8.

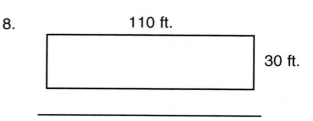

_____

Challenge

9. What is the perimeter of a rectangular room which is 25 feet long and 12 feet wide? _____

10. What is the perimeter of a rectangular building which is 45 meters long and 40 meters wide? _____

To compute the perimeter of a polygon, add the lengths of all sides.

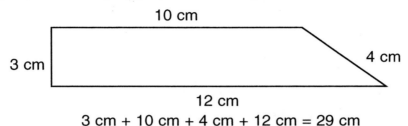

3 cm + 10 cm + 4 cm + 12 cm = 29 cm

Directions: Use the information on page 13 to help you compute the perimeter of these polygons. Remember to label the unit of measurement—feet, yards, centimeters, or meters—in your answer.

1.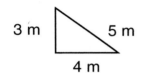

_____

2.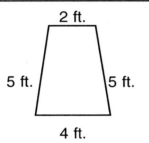

_____

3.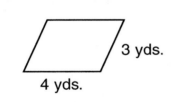

_____

4.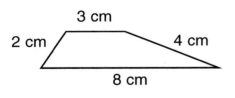

_____

5.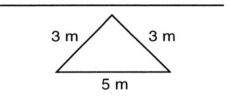

_____

6.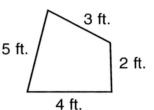

_____

7.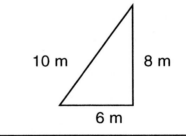

_____

8.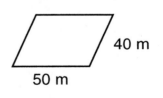

_____

Challenge

9. Measure how many small paper clips it would take to go all the way around this sheet of paper. _____

10. How many small paper clips would it take to go completely around your desk? _____

11. How could you do this same problem with only 1 small paper clip? _____

A rectangular house is 40 feet wide and 80 feet long. What is its perimeter?

40 ft.

80 ft.

Perimeter (P) of a rectangle = (l + w) x 2

P = (80 ft. + 40 ft.) x 2 = 240 feet

Directions: Use the information on page 13 to help you compute the perimeter. Remember to label the unit of measurement—feet—in your answer.

1. A bedroom is 10 feet wide and 20 feet long. What is the perimeter?

   _____

2. A rectangular house is 30 feet wide and 50 feet long. What is the perimeter?

   _____

3. A classroom is 18 feet wide and 20 feet long. What is the perimeter of the classroom?

   _____

4. A cafeteria is 60 feet long and 50 feet wide. What is the perimeter?

   _____

5. One wing of the Okie Dokie Elementary School is 100 feet long and 44 feet wide. Compute the perimeter.

   _____

6. A rectangular playing field at Okie Dokie Elementary School is 70 feet long and 20 feet wide. Compute the perimeter.

   _____

7. A rectangular fence around the school is 300 feet long and 140 feet wide. What is the perimeter?

   _____

8. A football field is 300 feet long from goal line to goal line and 160 feet wide from sideline to sideline. What is the perimeter of the field?

   _____

Challenge

9. Use a ruler to measure the length and width of your classroom. Compute the perimeter.

   _____

10. Use a yardstick to measure the length and width of the basketball court at school. Compute the perimeter.

    _____

11. Use a ruler to measure the length and width of your bedroom. Compute the perimeter.

    _____

Facts to Know

Area of Rectangles

- The area of a rectangle is computed by multiplying the length times the width.
- The formula is written: **A = l x w or Area = length x width**
- The answer is always given in square units. The word square and the units are usually abbreviated like this: 14 sq. m or 14 m^2

The rectangular figure represented here is 7 meters long and 2 meters wide.

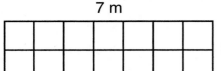

7 m

2 m

7 m x 2 m = 14 square meters or 14 sq. m or 14 m^2

Area of Squares

- Since a square has four equal sides, the area (A) of a square is computed by multiplying one side (s) of the square times itself.
- The formula is written: **A = s x s or A = s^2**
- The answer is always given in square units.

The square figure represented here has sides which are 4 yards long.

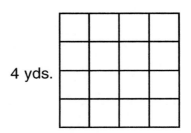

4 yds.

4 yards x 4 yards = 16 square yards

A = 16 sq. yds. or 16 yds.^{2}

Square Inch

- This is one square inch.
- All 4 sides are one inch long.

This figure is 5 inches long and 3 inches wide.

Use the square inch above to help you find out how many square inches this figure has.

You should have found 15 square inches. *Note: 5 in. x 3 in. = 15 sq. in.* When done, carefully cut out the square inches to use on the next page.

Directions: Use the information on page 17 and the 15 square inches cut out from that page to figure out how many square inches are in each shape.

1.

_____ square inches

2.

_____ square inches

3.

_____ square inches

4.

_____ square inches

5.

_____ square inches

6. Compute the area in square inches of a 3" by 5" index card. _____ square inches

7. Compute the area of a 4" by 6" index card. _____ square inches

8. Compute the area of a 5" by 8" index card. _____ square inches

Challenge

9. Compute the area of this paper. (Round off each side to the nearest inch.)
_____ square inches

This area of a rectangle is computed by multiplying the length (l) times the width (w). The formula is: **A = l x w**

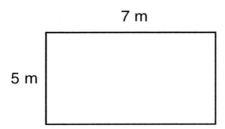

7 m

5 m

7 m x 5 m = 35 square meters
A = 35 sq. m or 35 m²

Directions: Use the information on page 17 to help you compute the areas of these figures. Remember to label the unit of measurement—square inches, square feet, square centimeters, square meters—in your answer.

1.

6 in.

3 in.

_____

2.

7 ft.

5 ft.

_____

3.

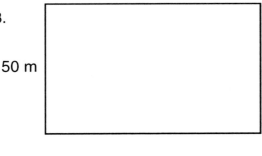

80 m

50 m

_____

4.

90 cm

20 cm

_____

5. What is the area of a rectangular room which is 12 feet long and 9 feet wide?_____

6. What is the area of a rectangular store which is 30 feet long and 20 feet wide?_____

7. What is the area of a table 6 feet long and 5 feet wide? _____

8. What is the area of a desk which is 40 inches long and 20 inches wide? _____

9. What is the area of a paper 28 centimeters long and 22 centimeters wide? _____

10. What is the area of a rectangular room which is 30 feet long and 12 feet wide?_____

The area of a square is computed by multiplying the length of one side of the square by itself. The formula is: **A = s x s** or **A = s²**

5 m

5 m x 5 m = 25 sq. m or 25 m²
Area = 25 square meters

Directions: Use the information on page 17 to help you compute the area of these squares. Remember to label the unit of measurement—square inches, square feet, square centimeters, square meters—in your answer.

1.

3 in.

_____

2.

4 m

_____

3.

6 ft.

_____

4.

7 m

_____

5.

60 m

_____

6.

50 m

_____

7. What is the area of a square table which is 30 inches long on each side?_____

8. What is the area of a square room which is 25 feet long on one side?_____

Facts to Know

Grams and Ounces

There are two common units of measurement for light objects.

- A *gram* is a metric unit. Scientists measure in grams. A large paper clip weighs about 1 gram.

- An *ounce* is a customary or English unit of measurement. It is equal to about 28 grams, which is approximately 28 large paper clips. Ounces are commonly used in daily life.

There are two types of instruments which might be used to measure light objects: an equal arm balance and a scale.

Equal Arm Balance

The *equal arm balance* compares the weight of a standard unit of measure, such as a gram weight or ounce weight, in one cup to the weight of an object in the other cup.

Use an equal arm balance to determine how many grams a pair of scissors weighs.

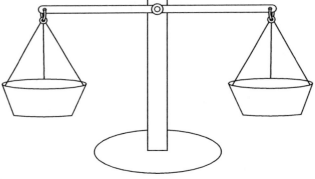

1. Use gram weights or large paper clips as weights. (Some large paper clips weigh a gram, and some weigh slightly more than a gram but are close enough for this activity.)

2. Place the object to be weighed—the scissors—in one cup. Place the gram weights—paper clips— in the other cup until the cups are equal or even with each other.

3. Count the weights or paper clips as you put them in the cup.

Scale

- A *scale*, such as a postal scale, indicates the weight of an object set on a tray of the scale by a series of marks indicating ounces or pounds.

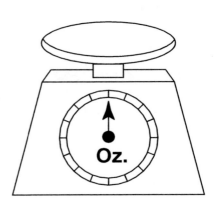

Use a small postal scale to weigh a box of crayons.

1. Put the crayon box on the tray.

2. Note where the indicator is pointing to determine the number of ounces.

Directions: Use a small scale, such as a postal scale, to weigh these items. Record their weights to the nearest ounce. (If no scale is available, estimate the number of ounces. Answers may vary.)

1. pair of glasses

   _____ ounces

2. full tissue box

   _____ ounces

3. dictionary

   _____ ounces

4. calculator

   _____ ounces

5. scissors

   _____ ounces

6. stapler

   _____ ounces

7. videotape

   _____ ounces

8. children's book

   _____ ounces

Directions: Use the information from the first activity to help you estimate the weights of these objects. Check your answers with a scale, if available.

9. thesaurus

   _____ ounces

10. 12 sheets of paper (8 ½" x 11")

    _____ ounces

11. field guide

    _____ ounces

12. encyclopedia (one book)

    _____ ounces

13. large pencil eraser

    _____ ounces

14. box of large paper clips

    _____ ounces

15. pad of paper

    _____ ounces

16. wallet

    _____ ounces

Directions: Find 5 objects in the classroom to weigh or estimate the weight.

Name of Object	Weight
_____	_____ ounces
_____	_____ ounces
_____	_____ ounces
_____	_____ ounces
_____	_____ ounces

A large paper clip weighs just about 1 gram. It can be used as a weight with an equal arm balance. Use the following procedure:

- Place the object to be weighed in one cup of the balance.
- Place large paper clips in the other cup until the two cups hang evenly.
- Count the paper clips as you place them in the cup.

Directions: Use an equal arm balance and large paper clips to weigh these items. Record their weights to the nearest gram. (If no balance is available, estimate the number of grams. Answers may vary.)

1. pencil

_____ grams

2. ruler

_____ grams

3. marker

_____ grams

4. crayon

_____ grams

5. protractor

_____ grams

6. key

_____ grams

7. penny

_____ grams

8. quarter

_____ grams

9. pen

_____ grams

10. large pencil eraser

_____ grams

Directions: Use the information from the first activity to help you estimate the weights of these objects. Check your answers with an equal arm balance, if available.

11. math compass

_____ grams

12. 1 sheet of paper (8 ½" x 11")

_____ grams

13. dime

_____ grams

14. plastic pencil sharpener

_____ grams

15. cassette

_____ grams

16. CD (compact disc)

_____ grams

17. computer diskette

_____ grams

18. 10 small paper clips

_____ grams

Directions: Use the information on page 21 to help you do this page. Use a scale to weigh these objects. Estimate weights if no scale is available.

1. 3 pencils

   _____ ounces

2. chalkboard eraser

   _____ ounces

3. CD (compact disc)

   _____ ounces

4. computer diskette

   _____ ounces

5. T-shirt

   _____ ounces

6. tennis ball

   _____ ounces

7. tennis shoe

   _____ ounces

8. yo-yo

   _____ ounces

9. math book

   _____ ounces

10. deck of cards

    _____ ounces

Directions: Use an equal arm balance and large paper clips to weigh these objects. Estimate weights if no balance is available.

11. 4 paper towels

    _____ grams

12. 1 small marble

    _____ grams

13. 10 rubber bands

    _____ grams

14. 1 jacks ball

    _____ grams

15. 1 piece of chalk

    _____ grams

16. 1 CD (compact disc)

    _____ grams

17. 1 computer diskette

    _____ grams

18. 1 watch

    _____ grams

19. Ping-Pong ball

    _____ grams

20. 1 checker game piece

    _____ grams

Directions: Find 4 other objects in the classroom to weigh or estimate the weight in either ounces or grams. Then record the measurement you used.

Name of Object	Weight
_____	_____ ounces or grams
_____	_____ ounces or grams
_____	_____ ounces or grams
_____	_____ ounces or grams

Facts to Know

- A pound is the customary unit of measurement for daily business in the United States.
- There are 16 ounces in 1 pound.
- There are 2,000 pounds in 1 ton.
- A scale is the most common instrument for measuring weights.

Sample A

A letter with 4 or 5 regular-sized (8 ½" x 11") pages and an envelope weigh 1 ounce. A pile of 16 similar letters weighs a pound. How many pounds would 32 letters weigh? Divide 32 letters by 16 ounces (1 pound).

$$16\overline{)32}^{\,2}$$

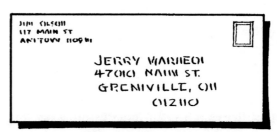

A pile of 32 letters would weigh about 2 pounds.

Sample B

One can of soup weighs 12 ounces. How many pounds would 4 cans of soup weigh? Multiply 4 cans x 12 ounces, which equals 48 ounces. Then divide 48 ounces by 16 ounces (1 pound).

$$16\overline{)48}^{\,3}$$

The 4 cans of soup weigh 3 pounds.

Sample C

Use a scale to weigh the following items:

- shoe
- paperback novel
- D cell battery
- box of tissue
- VCR tape

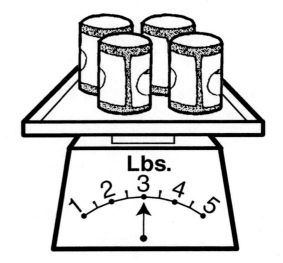

Which objects weigh closest to a pound? (Answers will vary depending on the size of the items.)

Directions: Use a scale, if available, to do these problems or make an estimate of the answer. Determine how many of the items listed below are needed to make one pound. (Get as close to a pound as you can.)

1. _____ boxes of small paper clips

6. _____ boxes of crayons

2. _____ boxes of large paper clips

7. _____ paperback books

3. _____ calculators

8. _____ CDs (compact discs)

4. _____ rulers

9. _____ computer diskettes

5. _____ pairs of scissors

10. _____ VCR cassettes

Directions: Use the information on page 25 to help you do these problems.

11. You ate 32 ounces of food for lunch. How many pounds did you eat?

_____ pounds

12. You have 48 ounces of paper. How many pounds of paper do you have?

_____ pounds

13. Your best friend was given 4 boxes of candy for his birthday. Each box was 12 ounces.

How many ounces of candy did your friend receive? _____ ounces

How many pounds of candy did your friend receive? _____ pounds

14. You found a treasure with 160 ounces of gold. How many pounds of gold did you find?
_____ pounds

15. Your principal bought 144 ounces of candy. How many pounds of candy did she buy?
_____ pounds

16. The soccer coach bought shoes which weighed 96 ounces. How many pounds did the shoes weigh? _____ pounds

Directions: Weigh the objects listed below on a scale, if available, or estimate the answer. Write the number of pounds and extra ounces for each item.

1. a quart of water

   _____ pounds and _____ ounces

2. an almanac

   _____ pounds and _____ ounces

3. one encyclopedia volume

   _____ pounds and _____ ounces

4. one brick

   _____ pounds and _____ ounces

5. a family-size can of soup

   _____ pounds and _____ ounces

6. a pair of tennis shoes

   _____ pounds and _____ ounces

7. a pair of jeans

   _____ pounds and _____ ounces

8. a bottle of soap

   _____ pounds and _____ ounces

9. a transistor radio

   _____ pounds and _____ ounces

10. a textbook

   _____ pounds and _____ ounces

Directions: Weigh each of the objects listed below on a scale, if available, or estimate the answer. Write the number of pounds and extra ounces for each item.

11. a baseball bat

   _____ pounds and _____ ounces

12. a basketball

   _____ pounds and _____ ounces

13. one gallon of water

   _____ pounds and _____ ounces

14. a football

   _____ pounds and _____ ounces

15. a bag of 100 marbles

   _____ pounds and _____ ounces

16. ten paperback books

   _____ pounds and _____ ounces

17. three boxes of tissue

   _____ pounds and _____ ounces

18. two rolls of paper towels

   _____ pounds and _____ ounces

19. ten decks of cards

   _____ pounds and _____ ounces

20. ten VCR cassettes

   _____ pounds and _____ ounces

Challenge

21. Compute the weight of everything in your desk. Weigh it in parts if necessary.

   _____ pounds and _____ ounces

22. Compute the weight of everything in your backpack (or a friend's).

   _____ pounds and _____ ounces

There are 2,000 pounds in 1 ton. If one brick weighs 2 pounds, how many bricks would weigh a ton?

$$2\overline{)2000}\ \ \ ^{1000}$$

Answer: 1,000 bricks

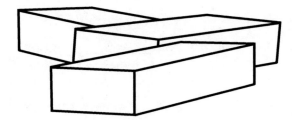

Directions: Use the information on page 25 to do the problems on this page. If your teacher approves, use a calculator to check your multiplication and division.

1. An airline traveler had 3 suitcases which weighed 200 pounds, 150 pounds, and 100 pounds. What was the total weight? _____

2. A bag of Sugar Drools Candy weighs 1 pound. How many bags would be in a ton of Sugar Drools Candy? _____

3. An almanac weighs 2 pounds. How many almanacs would a ton have?
_____

4. A VCR cassette weighs ½ of a pound. How many VCR cassettes would it take to make 10 pounds? _____

5. A paperback dictionary weighs 1 ½ pounds. How much would 10 paperback dictionaries weigh? _____

6. How much would 100 paperback dictionaries weigh? _____

7. A black bear weighs 500 pounds. How many black bears of the same weight would make a ton? _____

8. A bobcat weighs 50 pounds. How many bobcats of the same weight would make a ton?
_____

9. A badger weighs 25 pounds. How many badgers of the same weight would make a ton?
_____

10. How many pounds are in 5 tons? _____

Challenge: A set of encyclopedias has 25 books. Each book weighs 4 pounds. How many sets of encyclopedias would a ton hold? _____

Fact to Know

- The temperature on a thermometer is determined by finding the level of the red mercury in the tube and the number on the temperature scale across from it.
- The temperature is written in numbers with the ° sign. For example, 70° F is read: 70 degrees Fahrenheit.

Fahrenheit

- The Fahrenheit scale records the freezing point of water at 32° F and the boiling point of water at 212° F (at sea level).
- The temperature is usually reported in degrees Fahrenheit in newspapers, on the radio, and on television.

Celsius

- The Celsius scale is based on the freezing point of water at 0° C and a boiling point of water at 100° C (at sea level).
- The Celsius thermometer is usually used by scientists.

Here are the two thermometers:

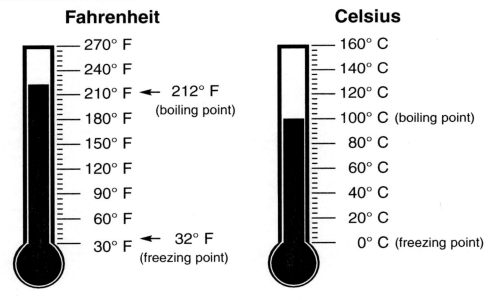

Sample A

A Fahrenheit thermometer has a reading of 68°, a normal room temperature. How much above freezing is this? To find the answer, subtract 32 (the freezing point of water) from 68.

$$\begin{array}{r} 68 \\ -\ 32 \\ \hline 36 \end{array}$$

The answer is 36 degrees above the freezing point of water, or 36° F.

Sample B

How many degrees below freezing is −10° F? Freezing is 32° F which is 32 degrees above 0° F. Add 10 more degrees (for the −10° F). The temperature is 42 degrees below freezing.

$$\begin{array}{r} 32 \\ +\ 10 \\ \hline 42 \end{array}$$

7 Practice •••••• Using a Fahrenheit Thermometer

Directions: Use the information on page 29 and a Fahrenheit scale thermometer, if available, to answer these questions.

1. What is the temperature at which water freezes? _____

2. What is the temperature at which water boils? _____

3. What temperature is 10 degrees above freezing? _____

4. What temperature is 70 degrees above freezing? _____

5. What temperature is 22 degrees below freezing? _____

6. How many degrees below freezing is 20° F? _____

7. How many degrees below freezing is 28° F? _____

8. Your body has a temperature of 98.6° F which is almost 99° F. About how many degrees above freezing is your body temperature? _____

9. A temperature of 0° F is 32 degrees below freezing. How many degrees below freezing is −10°F (10 below zero)? _____

10. How many degrees below freezing is −20° F (20 degrees below zero)? _____

11. How many degrees below freezing is −40° F (40 degrees below zero)? _____

12. The boiling point of water is 212° F. How many degrees below the boiling point is 100° F? _____

On Your Own

Use a thermometer to determine the temperature at your school or home this afternoon and tomorrow morning. Record the temperatures here.

This afternoon _____°F   Tomorrow morning _____°F

The reading on the thermometer on the right with the Celsius scale is 70° C.

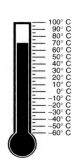

The thermometer on the right reads 10 degrees below zero (-10° C).

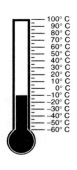

Directions: Use the information on page 29 to help you do these problems. Write down each thermometer reading in degrees Celsius.

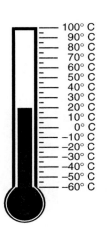

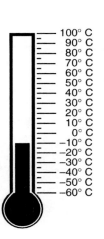

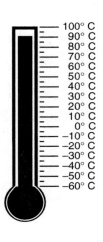

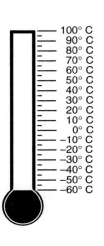

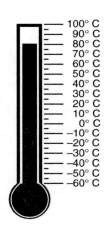

1. _____ 2. _____ 3. _____ 4. _____ 5. _____

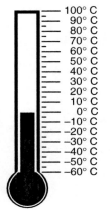

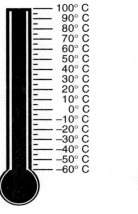

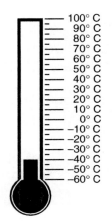

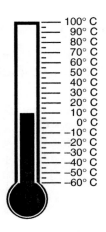

6. _____ 7. _____ 8. _____ 9. _____ 10. _____

 **Practice** •••••••••••• **Comparing Temperatures**

Directions: Use the information on page 29 and a Fahrenheit thermometer to do the problems on this page.

1. The highest recorded temperature in the United States was 134° F in California in 1913. The coldest recorded U.S. temperature was –80° F in Alaska in 1971. What is the difference between the two temperatures? _____

2. The highest recorded temperature in Europe was 122° F in Spain. The lowest recorded European temperature was in Russia at –67° F. What is the difference? _____

3. The highest recorded temperature in South America was 120° F in Argentina. The lowest recorded temperature in South America was –27° F in Argentina. What is the difference? _____

4. The highest recorded temperature in the world was 136° F in Libya, Africa, in 1922. The lowest recorded temperature was –129° F in Antarctica in 1983. What is the difference?

   _____

5. Asia's highest recorded temperature was 129° F in Israel. The lowest recorded temperature was –90° F in Russia. What is the difference? _____

On Your Own

Use a Fahrenheit thermometer to record the temperature twice a day at home or at school for one week.

Morning		**Afternoon**	
Time	Temperature	Time	Temperature
_____ A.M.	_____ ° F	_____ P.M.	_____ ° F
_____ A.M.	_____ ° F	_____ P.M.	_____ ° F
_____ A.M.	_____ ° F	_____ P.M.	_____ ° F
_____ A.M.	_____ ° F	_____ P.M.	_____ ° F
_____ A.M.	_____ ° F	_____ P.M.	_____ ° F

Internet Connection

Use the following Internet address listed here to check the temperatures in major cities around the United States or the world: http://www.temperatureworld.com

Select 5 cities. List the continent on which each city is located, and the high and low temperatures for one day.

City	Continent	High Temperature	Low Temperature
_____	_____	_____ ° F	_____ ° F
_____	_____	_____ ° F	_____ ° F
_____	_____	_____ ° F	_____ ° F
_____	_____	_____ ° F	_____ ° F
		_____ ° F	_____ ° F

Facts to Know

The most common small unit of liquid measurement for daily use is a fluid ounce.

- A fluid ounce (fl. oz.) is equal to 6 teaspoons (tsp.) full of liquid.

1 fluid ounce = 6 teaspoons

- A fluid ounce is equal to 30 milliliters. An eye dropper holds about 1 milliliter. It would take 30 eye droppers to hold 1 fluid ounce.

1 fluid ounce = 30 milliliters

Cups, Pints, Quarts, and Gallons

- There are 8 fluid ounces in 1 cup. (1 c. = 8 fl. oz.)

- There are 16 fluid ounces in 1 pint. (1 pt. = 16 fl. oz.)

- There are 32 fluid ounces in 1 quart. (1 qt. = 32 fl. oz.)

- There are 128 fluid ounces in 1 gallon. (1 gal. = 128 fl. oz.)

- There are 2 cups in 1 pint. (1 pt. = 2 c.)

- There are 2 pints in 1 quart. (1 qt. = 2 pts.)

- There are 4 quarts in 1 gallon. (1 gal. = 4 qts.)

Directions: Use the information on page 33 to help you do these problems.

How many teaspoons would it take to fill:

1. 1 fluid ounce _____

2. 2 fluid ounces _____

3. 4 fluid ounces _____

4. 8 fluid ounces _____

5. 5 fluid ounces _____

6. 12 fluid ounces _____

Directions: Use a 1-ounce cup to fill a variety of cups and bottles with water. Number the cups and bottles. Record the amount held by each cup or bottle.

7. _____ fluid ounces

8. _____ fluid ounces

9. _____ fluid ounces

10. _____ fluid ounces

11. _____ fluid ounces

12. _____ fluid ounces

13. _____ fluid ounces

14. _____ fluid ounces

Directions: Use the information on page 33 to help you do these problems.

15. How many fluid ounces are in 1 cup? _____ fl. oz.

16. How many fluid ounces would 3 cups hold? _____ fl oz.

17. How many fluid ounces would 4 cups hold? _____ fl. oz.

18. How many fluid ounces would 6 cups hold? _____ fl. oz.

19. How many fluid ounces would 8 cups hold? _____ fl. oz.

20. How many fluid ounces would 10 cups hold? _____ fl. oz.

21. How many fluid ounces would 40 cups hold? _____ fl. oz.

Directions: Use the information on page 33 to help you do these problems.

How many fluid ounces would it take to fill:

1. 1 cup   = _____ fluid ounces

2. 2 cups   = _____ fluid ounces

3. 3 cups   = _____ fluid ounces

4. 4 cups   = _____ fluid ounces

5. 5 cups   = _____ fluid ounces

6. 7 cups   = _____ fluid ounces

7. 8 cups   = _____ fluid ounces

8. 10 cups = _____ fluid ounces

9. A recipe for oatmeal requires 4 cups of water. How many fluid ounces of water are needed? _____ fl. oz.

10. A recipe for spaghetti requires 48 fluid ounces of water to cook the spaghetti. How many cups of water are needed? _____ cups

11. A pizza recipe requires 1 ½ cups of tomato sauce. How many fluid ounces of tomato sauce are needed? _____ fl. oz.

12. A recipe for chili calls for 2 quarts of water to cook the beans. How many fluid ounces are required? _____ fl. oz.

13. A recipe for soup for a Scout troop requires 2 gallons of water in which to boil the mix. How many fluid ounces are needed? _____ fl. oz.

14. The Scout troop also needs punch. The recipe calls for 5 cups of water. How many fluid ounces are in 5 cups? _____ fl. oz.

Challenge

15. A recipe calls for 1 gallon of water, 1 quart of milk, 1 pint of syrup, and 1 cup of juice. How many fluid ounces does the recipe require? _____ fl. oz.

16. A recipe calls for 2 gallons of milk, 2 quarts of soup broth, and 2 pints of water. How many fluid ounces does the recipe require? _____ fl. oz.

Directions: Use the information on page 33 to help you do these problems.

Record the correct amount of cups.

1. 1 quart = _____ cups

2. 2 quarts = _____ cups

3. 4 quarts = _____ cups

4. 1 gallon = _____ cups

5. 2 pints = _____ cups

6. 2 gallons   = _____ cups

7. ½ gallon   = _____ cups

8. 1 ½ gallons = _____ cups

9. 2 ½ quarts   = _____ cups

10. 5 pints   = _____ cups

Record the correct amount of pints.

11. 1 quart = _____ pints

12. 2 quarts = _____ pints

13. 3 quarts = _____ pints

14. 1 gallon = _____ pints

15. 7 quarts = _____ pints

16. 2 gallons   = _____ pints

17. ½ gallon   = _____ pints

18. 3 gallons   = _____ pints

19. 5 quarts   = _____ pints

20. 3 ½ quarts   = _____ pints

21. A lawn mower holds 1 ½ gallons of gas. How many quarts of gas does it hold?
_____ quarts

22. A motorized bike holds 2 ½ gallons of gas. How many quarts of gas can it hold?
_____ quarts

23. A small car holds 10 gallons of gas. How many pints does it hold? _____ pints

24. A large car holds 15 gallons of gas. How many pints does it hold? _____ pints

25. A truck with two tanks holds 40 gallons of gas. How many quarts does it hold?
_____ quarts

Challenge

26. A gasoline tanker has 9,000 gallons. How many quarts does it hold? _____ quarts

How many pints does it hold?_____ pints

Facts to Know

- There are 60 seconds in 1 minute.

- There are 60 minutes in 1 hour.

- There are 24 hours in 1 day.

- Time is measured on a clock in 12-hour segments.

- The short hand points to the hour. The long hand points to the minute.

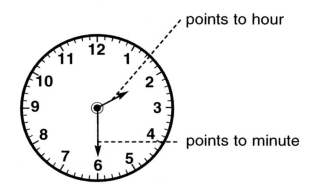

- Morning—A.M.—includes the hours from midnight to noon, from 12:00 A.M. through 11:59 A.M.

- Afternoon—P.M.—includes the hours from noon to midnight. The afternoon time is from 12:00 P.M. through 11:59 P.M.

 one minute after midnight

 one minute after noon

Computing Time

To compute elapsed time within the morning, subtract the smaller number from the higher one. Computing time within the afternoon is done the same way.

The time from 7:15 A.M. to 10:30 A.M. is done this way:

```
  10:30
-  7:15
```
3:15 (3 hours and 15 minutes)

The time from 6:35 P.M. to 9:00 P.M. is done this way:

```
   9:00
-  6:35
```
2:25 (2 hours and 25 minutes)

When going from A.M. to P.M. or from P.M. to A.M., you regroup 60 minutes (not 10 or 100).

The time from 9:00 P.M. to 6:30 A.M. is computed this way:

Step 1

```
12:00 midnight
-  9:00
   3:00 hrs.
```

Step 2

```
  3:00 (Add)
+ 6:30 (12:00 midnight to 6:30 A.M. is 6 hrs. and 30 min.)
  9:30 (9 hours and 30 minutes)
```

Directions: Write the time shown on these clock faces. *Reminder:* The short hand points to the hour. The long hand points to the minute.

1.

_____

2.

_____

3.

_____

4.

_____

5.

_____

6.

_____

7.

_____

8.

_____

9.

_____

Directions: Make the clock face match the digital read-out. Use a shorter mark for the hour hand and a longer mark for the minute hand. The first one is done for you.

10.

5:15

11.

9:30

12.

6:45

13.

10:50

14.

8:25

15.

3:20

Directions: Use the clues to decide whether the time shown on these clock faces are for A.M. or P.M. Circle A.M. or P.M.

Remember: Morning—A.M.—includes the hours from midnight to noon (12:00 A.M. through 11:59 A.M.). Afternoon—P.M.—includes the hours from noon to midnight (12:00 P.M. through 11:59 P.M.).

1. School begins

A.M.   P.M.

2. Homework time

A.M.   P.M.

3. Birthday party

5:00

A.M.   P.M.

4. Wake-up alarm

A.M.   P.M.

5. Afternoon snack

3:50

A.M.   P.M.

6. Dinnertime

A.M.   P.M.

7. Lunchtime

A.M.   P.M.

8. Afternoon nap

A.M.   P.M.

9. Morning shower

7:05

A.M.   P.M.

10. Stores open

9:00

A.M.   P.M.

11. Stores close

A.M.   P.M.

12. Pizza dinner

A.M.   P.M.

How long is it from 10:00 A.M. to 2:30 P.M.?
Subtract 10:00 from 12:00. This equals 2 hours.
2:30 P.M. is 2 ½ hours after noon.
Add 2 hours + 2 ½ hours = 4 ½ hours.
The answer is 4 ½ hours.

```
   12:00
 − 10:00
 ───────
   2:00
 + 2:30
 ───────
   4:30
```

Directions: Use the information on page 37 to help you compute these times.
How much time is there between:

1. 7:00 A.M. and 10:15 A.M.

_____

2. 3:00 A.M. and 6:45 A.M.

_____

3. 9:00 P.M. and 11:30 P.M.

_____

4. 6:00 P.M. and 10:45 P.M.

_____

5. 8:15 A.M. and 11:50 A.M.

_____

6. 4:15 P.M. and 10:40 P.M.

_____

7. 7:30 A.M. and 10:00 A.M.

_____

8. 4:30 P.M. and 11:00 P.M.

_____

9. 3:45 P.M. and 6:00 P.M.

_____

10. 8:55 A.M. and 10:00 A.M.

_____

11. 7:45 P.M. and 10:15 P.M.

_____

12. 2:30 A.M. and 8:00 A.M.

_____

13. 9:45 A.M. and 12:00 noon

_____

14. 7:50 P.M. and 12:00 midnight

_____

Directions: Try these. Remember to borrow 60 minutes (not 10 or 100) when you need to borrow time.

15. 10:00 A.M. and 1:00 P.M.

_____

16. 7:00 A.M. and 3:00 P.M.

_____

17. 9:00 P.M. and 4:00 A.M.

_____

18. 11:00 P.M. and 6:30 A.M.

_____

19. 4:00 P.M. and 5:00 A.M.

_____

20. 8:00 A.M. and 6:45 P.M.

_____

Challenge: How much time is there between 5:36 P.M. and 11:52 A.M.?_____

Speed is usually measured in terms of the distance traveled and the time it takes to travel that distance. Look at the following example:

Joseph rode his bike 1 mile in 10 minutes.

How many miles could he travel in 60 minutes at that speed?

To find the answer, divide 10 into 60 to get 6.

$$10 \overline{)60} \quad \stackrel{6}{}$$

Joseph rides his bike at a speed of 6 miles per hour (m.p.h.).

Directions: Compute the speeds indicated here.

1. Anna rides her bike 1 mile in 12 minutes. At that speed, how many miles can she ride in 1 hour? _____ miles

2. Juanita walks 1 mile in 15 minutes. At that speed, how many miles can she walk in 1 hour? _____ miles

3. The track coach can run 1 mile in 6 minutes. At that speed, how many miles can he run in 1 hour? _____ miles

4. Your best friend walked 1 mile in 10 minutes. At that speed, how many miles could your friend walk in 1 hour? _____ miles

5. Your teacher drove 15 miles in 30 minutes. At that speed, how far would she travel in 1 hour? _____ miles

Directions: Compare these speeds.

6. A domestic (pet) cat can run 30 miles per hour for a short distance. A lion can run 50 miles per hour for a short distance. How many miles per hour faster is the lion? _____ miles per hour

7. At its maximum speed over a short distance, a grizzly bear can run 30 miles per hour. A gray fox can run a short distance at 42 miles per hour. How many miles per hour faster is the fox? _____ miles per hour

8. A cheetah can run for a short distance at 70 miles per hour. A horse can run 47 miles per hour for a short distance. How many miles per hour faster is the cheetah? _____ miles per hour

Challenge

9. A bicyclist travels 100 miles in 10 hours. How many miles would she travel in 1 hour? _____ miles

10. A bicyclist traveled 3,200 miles across the United States. He traveled 100 miles a day every day. How many days did it take him to complete the ride? _____ days

Jodelle drove her car 400 miles in 8 hours.
What was her speed in miles per hour?
Divide 400 miles by the time, 8 hours.

$$8 \overline{)\ 400}^{\ \ 50}$$

The answer is Jodelle drove 50 miles per hour (m.p.h.).

Directions: Compute these speeds in miles per hour (m.p.h.).

1. You and your cousin went in-line skating for 4 hours and traveled 12 miles. What was your average speed? _____ miles per hour

2. You took a skateboarding outing with a good friend. You went 14 miles in 7 hours. What was your average speed? _____ miles per hour

3. Your principal took a tour of the desert. She traveled 120 miles in 3 hours. What was her average speed? _____ miles per hour

4. Your friend won a trip to an amusement park in another state. Your friend traveled 160 miles in 4 hours. What was his average speed? _____ miles per hour

5. You won a bus tour through three states. You traveled 600 miles in 20 hours. What was your bus's average speed? _____ miles per hour

6. You and your family take a bike vacation. You travel 300 miles in 60 hours of biking. What was your average speed? _____ miles per hour

7. Your favorite teacher drove across country for a summer vacation. She traveled 3,200 miles and drove 80 hours. What was her average speed? _____ miles per hour

8. You took a 4-hour horseback ride across the plains for 60 miles. What was your average speed? _____ miles per hour

Challenge

9. Two Eagle Scouts walked across the United States traveling 3,600 miles. They walked a total of 900 hours. What was their average speed? _____ miles per hour

10. Two Girl Scouts walked 2,400 miles from Texas to Washington state. They walked a total of 600 hours. What was their average speed? _____ miles per hour

There are 7 days in 1 week. There are 52 weeks in 1 year.
There are 12 months in 1 year. There are 365 days in 1 year.

April, June, September, and November have 30 days. All the rest of the months have 31 days except for February which has 28 days (and 29 days in a leap year).

Sun.	Mon.	Tues.	Wed.	Thurs.	Fri.	Sat.
	1	2	3	4	5	6
7	8	9	10	11	12	13
14	15	16	17	18	19	20
21	22	23	24	25	26	27
28	29	30	31			

Directions: Use the information listed above and the calendar to answer these questions.

1. How many full 7-day weeks beginning on Sunday are in this month? _____

2. How many Fridays are in this month? _____

3. How many Sundays are in this month? _____

4. How many days are in this month? _____

5. If you have an appointment one week after the 15th, what is the date and the day of the week? Date _____ Day of the week _____

6. What will be the date and day of the week one week after the 31st?

   Date _____ Day of the week _____

7. Could this month be February? _____ Explain your answer. _____

8. Could this month be June? _____ Explain your answer. _____

9. Could this month be July? _____ Explain your answer. _____

10. If you have a game two weeks from the 17th, what is the date and day of the week?

    Date _____ Day of the week _____

Challenge: What is the date and day of the week 3 weeks from the 29th?

   Date _____ Day of the week _____

> There are 12 months in 1 year. There are 52 weeks in 1 year.
>
> There are 365 days in 1 year. Leap year—every 4th year—has 366 days.

Directions: Use the information from this page to answer these questions.

1. If you are 8 years old, through how many leap years would you have lived?
_____

2. The year is often divided into 4 quarters. In what month would the second quarter begin? _____

3. In what month would the third quarter begin? _____

4. In what month would the fourth quarter begin? _____

5. How many weeks would be in each quarter? _____

6. About how many days would be in each quarter? _____

7. If your grandfather was 80 years old, through how many leap years would he have lived?
_____

8. How many days would a president serve if he was president for one full four-year term?
_____

9. How many days of the year are left after the 1st of December? _____

10. How many days are in 12 weeks? _____

Challenge

11. What day of the 366-day year is the 29th of February? _____

12. How many days of the year are left after February 29th? _____

13. What day of the year does July 4 occur? (2 possible answers) _____

14. How many days of the year are left after July 4? _____

15. What is the highest number of leap years through which a 25-year-old person could have lived? _____

Before the Computer

- If you have a printer and a drawing program, such as *ClarisWorks®* or *MSWorks®*, you can create your own metric ruler for use in the following activity. You will need to have some experience using the drawing program. If not, an assistant may be needed to guide you through steps in this activity.

- You need to understand the difference between metric measurements and standard measurements, which are still used in the United States.

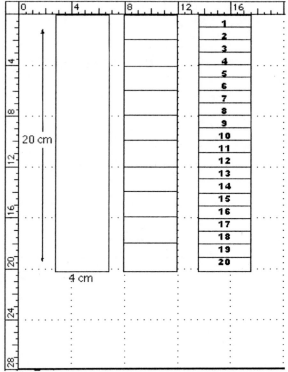

On the Computer

- Start the drawing application and turn on the ruler function. If you are using *MSWorks*, find the ruler function in the View pull-down menu.

- Change the measurement units on the ruler. The drawing page will be in inches since this is the unit most commonly used. If you are working with *ClarisWorks*, find Rulers under the Format pull-down menu.

- Set the units to centimeters. If you have difficulty at this step and do not know where to make these changes, ask one of the classroom experts for help.

- You should now see rulers in centimeters on both the top and left or right edges, depending on which program is being used.

- Most drawing programs have a View button. This button, which can be found in a menu, will allow you to shrink or enlarge the screen. Shrink or scale the picture to 50%. This will allow you to see the entire page, and that will make drawing the ruler much easier.

- The picture shows the three steps needed in order to make a metric ruler. First, draw a rectangle that is 4 centimeters (cm) wide and 20 centimeters (cm) long.

- Next, add divisions that are 2 cm apart. If the program being used has an autogrid function, use it to draw the lines.

- Finally, draw lines at 1 cm intervals. Notice that on the left-hand ruler, the first number found is 4. On the ruler being created, there should be 4 cm when you reach this point.

- After having completed marking off all the 1-cm intervals on the ruler, label them. This can be done either before printing or after.

- Rulers should measure exactly 20 cm. Check it against another metric ruler in the classroom.

You are now ready to complete the activity on the following page!

Finding the Measurement

- You are now ready to measure a variety of items in the classroom once you have completed the activity on page 45. The following is a list of items that you will be measuring. Before starting, make some predictions about how many centimeters these items are. You may want to devise a plan that you can use to measure items that are more than 20 cm long.

- Use the ruler that you created to measure the objects listed. Fill in the chart below as you go along. When you are done measuring all of the objects, complete the assessment questions below.

Item	Predicted Size	Actual Size
a. your math book ⟶		
b. your pencil ⟶		
c. the top of your desk ⟶		
d. your little finger ⟶		
e. the chalkboard ⟶		
f. your shoe ⟶		
g. any ball ⟶		
h. a crayon ⟶		
I. a piece of notebook paper ⟶		

Assessment

This is a self-assessment activity. Answer the following questions.

1. What part of the activity did you find most difficult?_____

   _____

2. How many of the items were larger than 20 cm? What did you have to do in order to measure those items? _____

   _____

3. Do you think that everyone doing this activity will come up with the same kind of results that you did? _____ Why or why not?_____

   _____

   _____

Page 6
1. 2 inches
2. 1 ½ inches
3. 2 inches
4. 2 ½ inches
5. Answers will vary.
6. Answers will vary.
7. Answers will vary.
8. Answers will vary.

Page 7
Answers will vary.

Page 8
Answers will vary.

Page 10
1. 5 ⅞ inches
2. 2 ⅝ inches
3. 3 ⅜ inches or 3 ¼ inches
4. 2 ⅞ inches
5. Answers will vary.
6. Answers will vary.
7. Answers will vary.
8. Answers will vary.
9. Answers will vary.
10. Answers will vary.
11. Answers will vary.
12. Answers will vary.

Page 11
1. 1 ¾ + 1 ½ = 3 ¼ inches
2. 1 ¾ + 2 ½ = 4 ¼ inches
3. ⅞ + 1 ⅞ inches = 2 ⅝ inches or 2 ¾ inches
4. 3 - 1 ½ = 1 ½ inch
5. 3 ½ - ⅛ = 3 ⅜ inches

Page 12
1. 7 cm, 70 mm
2. 3 ½ cm, 35 mm
3. 2 ½ cm, 25 mm
4. 5 cm, 50 mm
5. 8 cm, 80 mm
6. 2 cm, 20 mm
7. 7 cm, 70 mm
8. 5 cm, 50 mm

Page 14
1. 22 yds.
2. 24 m
3. 220 m
4. 220 m
5. 22 in.
6. 30 ft.
7. 140 yds.
8. 280 ft.
9. 74 ft.
10. 170 m

Page 15
1. 12 m
2. 16 ft.
3. 14 yds.
4. 17 cm
5. 14 ft.
6. 11 m
7. 24 m
8. 180 m
9. Answers will vary.
10. Answers will vary.
11. Answers will vary.

Page 16
1. 60 ft.
2. 160 ft.
3. 76 ft.
4. 220 ft.
5. 288 ft.
6. 180 ft.
7. 880 ft.
8. 920 ft.
9. Answers will vary.
10. Answers will vary.
11. Answers will vary.

Page 18
1. 2 sq. in.
2. 3 sq. in.
3. 4 sq. in.
4. 6 sq. in.
5. 12 sq. in.
6. 15 sq. in.
7. 24 sq. in.
8. 40 sq. in.
9. 99 sq. in.

Page 19
1. 18 sq. in.
2. 35 sq. ft.
3. 4,000 sq. m
4. 1,800 sq. cm
5. 108 sq. ft.
6. 600 sq. ft.
7. 30 sq. ft.
8. 800 sq. in.
9. 616 sq. cm
10. 360 sq. ft.

Page 20
1. 9 sq. in.
2. 16 sq. m
3. 36 sq. ft.
4. 49 sq. m
5. 3,600 sq. m
6. 2,500 sq. m
7. 900 sq. in.
8. 625 sq. ft.

Page 22
Answers will vary.

Page 23
Answers will vary.

Page 24
Answers will vary.

Page 26
Answers will vary on 1–10.
11. 2 pounds
12. 3 pounds
13. 48 ounces; 3 pounds
14. 10 pounds
15. 9 pounds
16. 6 pounds

Page 27
Answers will vary.

Page 28
1. 450 lbs.
2. 2,000 bags
3. 1,000 almanacs
4. 20 VCR cassettes
5. 15 lbs.
6. 150 lbs.
7. 4 black bears
8. 40 bobcats
9. 80 badgers
10. 10,000 lbs.
Challenge: 20 sets

Page 30
1. 32° F
2. 212° F
3. 42° F
4. 102° F
5. 10° F
6. 12° F
7. 4° F
8. 67° F
9. 42° F
10. 52° F
11. 72° F
12. 112° F

Page 31
1. 20° C
2. -10° C
3. 90° C
4. -60° C
5. 80° C
6. 0° C
7. 100° C
8. 70° C
9. -40° C
10. 10° C

Page 32
1. 214° F
2. 189° F
3. 147° F
4. 265° F
5. 219° F

Page 34
1. 6 tsp.
2. 12 tsp.
3. 24 tsp.
4. 48 tsp.
5. 30 tsp.
6. 72 tsp.
7. Answers will vary.
8. Answers will vary.
9. Answers will vary.
10. Answers will vary.
11. Answers will vary.
12. Answers will vary.
13. Answers will vary.
14. Answers will vary.
15. 8 fl. oz.
16. 24 fl. oz.
17. 32 fl. oz.
18. 48 fl. oz.
19. 64 fl. oz.
20. 80 fl. oz.
21. 320 fl. oz.

Page 35
1. 8 fl. oz.
2. 16 fl. oz.
3. 24 fl. oz.
4. 32 fl. oz.
5. 40 fl. oz.
6. 56 fl. oz.
7. 64 fl. oz.
8. 80 fl. oz.
9. 32 fl. oz.
10. 6 cups
11. 12 fl. oz.
12. 64 fl. oz.
13. 256 fl. oz.
14. 40 fl. oz.
15. 184 fl. oz.
16. 352 fl. oz.

Page 36
1. 4 cups
2. 8 cups
3. 16 cups
4. 16 cups
5. 4 cups
6. 32 cups
7. 8 cups
8. 24 cups
9. 10 cups
10. 10 cups
11. 2 pints
12. 4 pints
13. 6 pints
14. 8 pints
15. 14 pints
16. 16 pints
17. 4 pints
18. 24 pints
19. 10 pints
20. 7 pints
21. 6 quarts
22. 10 quarts
23. 80 pints
24. 120 pints
25. 160 quarts
26. 36,000 quarts; 72,000 pints

Page 38
1. 6:05
2. 6:15
3. 12:00
4. 5:10
5. 11:30
6. 8:45
7. 3:20
8. 9:35
9. 2:50

10.   13.

11.   14.

12. 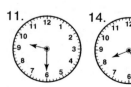   15.

Page 39
1. A.M.
2. P.M.
3. P.M.
4. A.M.
5. P.M.
6. P.M.
7. P.M.
8. P.M.
9. A.M.
10. A.M.
11. P.M.
12. P.M.

Page 40
1. 3 hr. 15 min.
2. 3 hr. 45 min.
3. 2 hr. 30 min.
4. 4 hr. 45 min.
5. 3 hr. 35 min.
6. 6 hr. 25 min.
7. 2 hr. 30 min.
8. 6 hr. 30 min.
9. 2 hr. 15 min.
10. 1 hr. 5 min.
11. 2 hr. 30 min.
12. 5 hr. 30 min.
13. 2 hr. 15 min.
14. 4 hr. 10 min.
15. 3 hr.
16. 8 hr.
17. 7 hr.
18. 7 hr. 30 min.
19. 13 hr.
20. 10 hr. 45 min.
Challenge: 18 hr. 16 min.

Page 41
1. 5 miles
2. 4 miles
3. 10 miles
4. 6 miles
5. 30 miles
6. 20 m.p.h. faster
7. 12 m.p.h. faster
8. 23 m.p.h. faster
9. 10 miles
10. 32 days

Page 42
1. 3 m.p.h.
2. 2 m.p.h.
3. 40 m.p.h.
4. 40 m.p.h.
5. 30 m.p.h.
6. 5 m.p.h.
7. 40 m.p.h.
8. 15 m.p.h.
9. 4 m.p.h.
10. 4 m.p.h.

Page 43
1. 3 weeks
2. 4 Fridays
3. 4 Sundays
4. 31 days
5. 22; Monday
6. 7; Wednesday
7. No; it has too many days
8. No; June has only 30 days
9. Yes; July has 31 days
10. 31; Wednesday
Challenge: 19; Monday

Page 44
1. 2 leap years
2. April
3. July
4. October
5. 13 weeks
6. 91 days
7. 20 leap years
8. 1,461 days
9. 30 days
10. 84 days
11. 60th day
12. 306 days
13. 185th or 186th day
14. 180 days
15. 7 leap years

Page 46
Answers will vary.